JOBS IN

HEALTH

PETER TURNER

WORKING IN AUSTRALIA

REDBACK publishing

First published 2022 by
Redback Publishing
Australia

www.redbackpublishing.com.au
orders@redbackpublishing.com.au

ISBN 978-1-761400-35-3 PBK

Author: Peter Turner
Editor: Caroline Thomas
Designer: Redback Publishing

Original illustrations © Redback Publishing 2024
Originated by Redback Publishing

A catalogue record for this book is available from the National Library of Australia

Acknowledgements
Abbreviations: l—left, r—right, b—bottom, t—top, c—centre, m—middle
We would like to thank the following for permission to reproduce photographs: (Images © shutterstock)

p5br, Malcolm P Chapman / Shutterstock.com ,
p8t, Shane White / Shutterstock.com ,
p9t borisoot wattanarat / Shutterstock.com,
p26l ARM Photo Video / Shutterstock.com,
p26b, Travelling.About / Shutterstock.com,
p27m ARM Photo Video / Shutterstock.com,
27b ArliftAtoz2205 / Shutterstock.com,

CONTENTS

WORKING IN THE HEALTH SERVICES

People employed in health occupations include doctors, dentists, nurses, physiotherapists, medical technologists, ambulance workers, pharmacists and educators.

WORK TYPES

KEY AREAS IN HEALTH

- DOCTORS AND SPECIALISTS
- NURSING AND PATIENT CARE
- PHARMACEUTICALS
- MEDICAL TECHNOLOGY

There are many exciting jobs within each of these different types of health services.

QUALIFICATIONS

The various jobs and careers in health all require their own qualifications and training. Most jobs in health also allow for specialisation within a field. Some people enter an occupation at a junior level and gradually gain higher levels of qualifications to move into a job with greater responsibility and a higher income.

Some jobs in health can start immediately after completing high school, with training delivered on-the-job, but most health occupations require a tertiary qualification. Some courses require particular study paths and almost all entry level roles require high grades.

GAINING A JOB

There are usually many people applying for the same occupation vacancy. To be successful in gaining a job you are likely to need more than the minimum level of qualifications required, to stand out over other applicants.

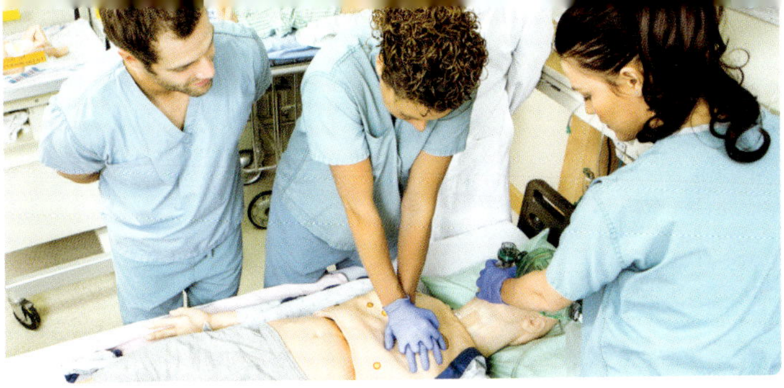

HIGH STANDARDS

Australia's high standard of health care not only requires sophisticated medical science and technology, but caring and well-trained workers. Health professionals must be passionate about helping people. For many workers, the greatest reward for their work is the ability to assist people when they really need it. Some workers, such as ambulance officers, have short, intense contact with patients. Doctors and dentists can have continued contact with patients over many years.

WORKING OVERSEAS

People who have completed the high standard of Australian training for health occupations are very well regarded overseas and can usually find work in English speaking countries. There are also opportunities for both paid and voluntary work with aid agencies such as the Red Cross and agencies of the United Nations.

DOCTORS AND SPECIALISTS

Both general practitioners and specialists can work in hospitals or in private practices. If a health problem continues for some time, or if it requires more detailed knowledge or experience, a GP will usually refer the patient to a specialist. Many specialists divide their time between private practices and work in hospitals.

GENERAL PRACTITIONER

JOB DESCRIPTION

General practitioners usually work in a clinic or medical centre where they see several patients each day. They require a broad and thorough knowledge of the human body to be able to give health advice, prescribe appropriate medications and manage patients' health problems.

RANGE OF WORK:

- diagnose a very wide range of medical illnesses, conditions and injuries
- treat a wide range of people including babies, children, teenagers, adults and the elderly
- perform minor surgery such as suturing and removing in-grown toenails

EDUCATION AND TRAINING

To become a general practitioner you must complete a medical degree at university. To be accepted to study a medical degree you must achieve very good marks at Year 12 and usually sit a separate, university entrance exam as well. A medical degree can take up to six years to complete, then to work as a doctor, you also need to complete an internship. GPs need a wide range of medical experience and must complete extra study.

SPECIALISTS

JOB DESCRIPTION

A specialist has more detailed knowledge about a particular area of medicine, often associated with a specific area of the body, or a specific skill.

RANGE OF SPECIALITIES:

- **surgeon** – perform operations on patients
- **anaesthetist** – administer medication to patients to sedate them ready for surgery
- **neurologist** – treat injuries and diseases of the brain, spinal chord and nerves
- **dermatologist** – treat skin problems
- **obstetrician** – provide medical care for women during pregnancy and childbirth
- **ear, nose and throat specialist** – treat medical conditions of the ears, nose and throat
- **cardiologist** – treat conditions of the heart
- **paediatrician** – treat medical problems in babies and children
- **gastroenterologist** – treat problems and conditions of the digestive system
- **ophthalmologist** – treat eye diseases and problems, and operates on the eyes

EDUCATION AND TRAINING

To become a specialist you must have already finished a medical degree. Then, you have to study and undergo training in your chosen speciality for a number of years and pass specialist exams. The number of years of study varies, depending on the speciality and the number of specialists permitted to pass each year.

'if you don't like working with people, you won't enjoy being a GP.'

MY STORY

I enjoy working as a general practitioner because I can treat a whole range of patients, from newborn babies to the elderly. Some of my patients were babies when I first met them and now they are teenagers. It's really nice to know, help and stay with my patients as they grow and change. I have always enjoyed science and became interested in studying medicine when I was in high school. I decided that being a general practitioner would provide the most variety.

I have worked in several hospitals as part of my training and I have been a partner in a medical practice for 10 years. We have seven doctors in our surgery and we all work part-time so that we can combine being parents with being doctors. We also have other health professionals working with us, including a physiotherapist, a dietitian, a psychologist and a massage therapist.

A few words of advice:
To be a GP you need to enjoy and be interested in working with lots of different people every day. You might get great marks at university, but if you don't like working with people, you won't enjoy being a GP.

NATALIE TAFT
GENERAL PRACTITIONER

NURSES

A career in nursing offers a variety of job opportunities and working environments. There are many different places nurses can work, including city or country hospitals, the army, maternal and child health centres, prisons, aged-care centres, international aid agencies and at community events.

NURSE

JOB DESCRIPTION

Nurses usually work as part of a team of health care professionals that includes doctors, specialists, and other health practitioners such as physiotherapists. Within this team nurses play an important role as a link between patients, their families and other health professionals.

RANGE OF WORK:

- supervise or administer medications and treatments that have been prescribed by doctors or other health professionals
- care for patients' physical and emotional needs
- monitor, observe, record and report on patients' conditions and any reactions they may have to treatments or medications
- discuss treatments and medications with patients and their families
- help patients move around
- assist with patients' rehabilitation activities

EDUCATION AND TRAINING

Nursing requires the completion of a university degree and extensive on-the-job training. There are a range of nursing degrees, each with different areas of focus. To be accepted into a degree course in nursing you need to have passed Year 12.

SPECIALIST NURSES

JOB DESCRIPTION

Like other health professionals, nurses can choose to do extra training to specialise in the care of a specific group of people.

RANGE OF SPECIALITIES:

- **adolescent health** – help young people with their emotional and physical needs
- **theatre** – work in operating theatres
- **palliative care** – care for patients who cannot be cured
- **midwifery** – help mothers before, during and after giving birth
- **neo-natal intensive care** – care for newborn babies who are sick or who were born premature
- **drug and alcohol care** – work with patients who have problems with alcohol or drug abuse
- **emergency care** – treat patients in the emergency department of a hospital

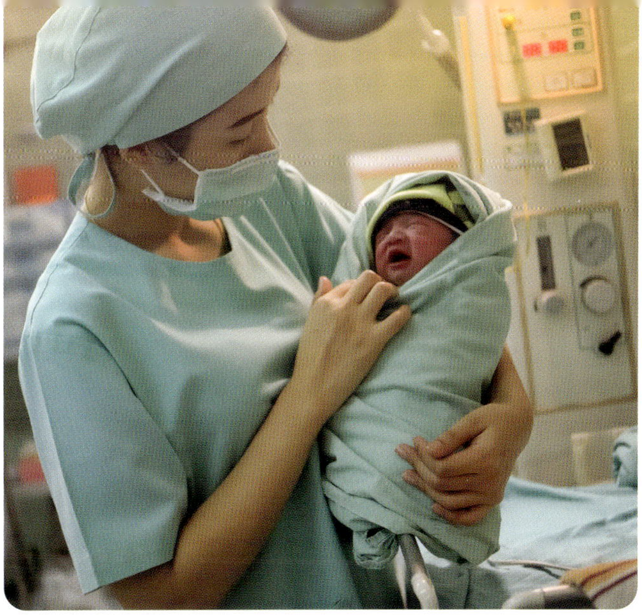

EDUCATION AND TRAINING

There are many opportunities for nurses to gain further training in order to move into various specialities throughout their career. This training is usually on the job, involving supervision by specialists, together with formal lectures. Postgraduate qualifications are needed for some positions.

MY STORY

'Nursing is a very flexible career ... Keep trying different areas'

I decided to be a nurse when I was in Year 11 at school. My aunt was a nurse and she used to tell me about the fun she had with the people she worked with – other nurses, doctors and patients.

After finishing my training I worked as a general staff nurse at the Alfred Hospital in Melbourne for 12 months, then I started training in midwifery. During my career I have trained and worked in several areas including midwifery, paediatrics, home care, coronary care, occupational health and safety and diabetes education. Some of the changes I've made have been because I wanted more variety or to try a new area after working at a speciality for a couple of years. I've also made changes because of the working hours involved.

A few words of advice:
Nursing is a very flexible career so you don't need to get stuck in one area. Keep trying different areas so you get broad experience.

PRUE ROBERTSON
NURSE

ASSISTING PATIENTS AND NURSES

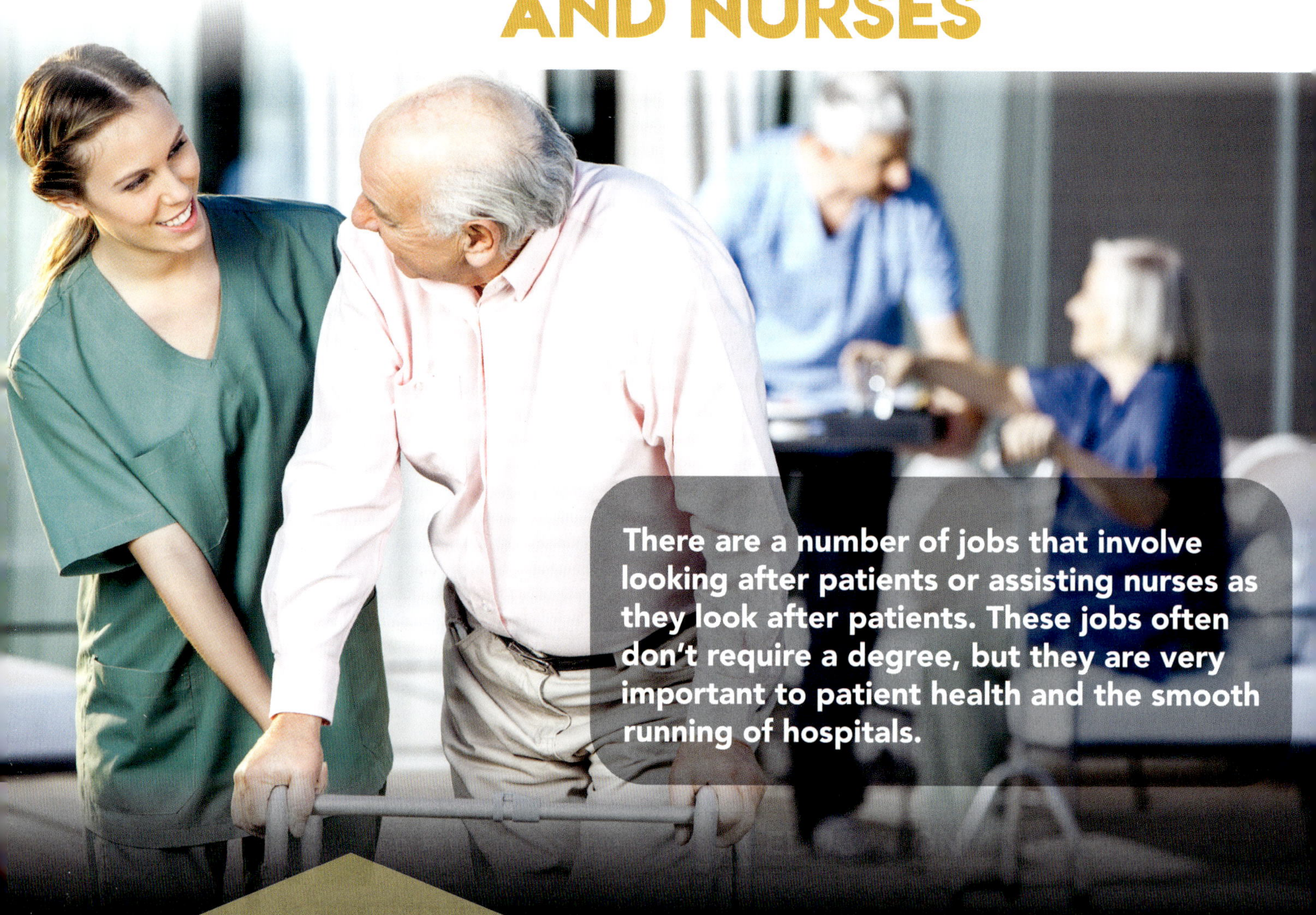

There are a number of jobs that involve looking after patients or assisting nurses as they look after patients. These jobs often don't require a degree, but they are very important to patient health and the smooth running of hospitals.

NURSING ASSISTANTS

JOB DESCRIPTION

Nursing assistants, also known as personal care assistants, provide assistance to nursing staff in non-medical, personal care, such as helping patients to wash, dress, shave, eat and communicate. Nursing assistants work in all areas of nursing, but most jobs are in hospitals, aged care and disability care services.

EDUCATION AND TRAINING

It is possible to get a job as a nursing assistant without any training and then be trained on-the-job, but many nursing assistants have qualifications in personal care from TAFE colleges.

WARD ASSISTANT

JOB DESCRIPTION

Ward assistants assist nurses and other health care providers in hospitals. They are not involved in medical or treatment duties but are general assistants who help to maintain a comfortable environment for patients.

RANGE OF WORK:

- transport patients around the hospital
- supply clean linen and towels
- distribute food and collect empty food trays
- clean ward equipment such as bedpans, bowls and buckets
- clean floors and furniture in patients' rooms

EDUCATION AND TRAINING

Many ward assistants don't have formal qualifications and receive on-the-job training. Some have completed certificate courses in patient services at TAFE colleges.

WARD CLERK

JOB DESCRIPTION

Ward clerks work in various departments of a hospital as a first contact for patients coming to hospital for treatment. The ward clerk acts like a receptionist and is usually the first person a patient meets when they come to hospital. A ward clerk will often have to deal with people who are anxious or upset, so they need to enjoy working with people.

RANGE OF WORK:

- arrange appointments
- greet the patients when they arrive
- take down personal details from the patients
- processing paperwork
- liaise between patients and the medical staff

EDUCATION AND TRAINING

There is no specialised training to become a ward clerk, although computer skills would be an advantage. Ward clerks have often worked in other assistant roles in a hospital and trained on-the-job.

MY STORY

I enjoy meeting lots of different people every day. As a ward clerk I'm the first person patients meet when they come to hospital. Often, the patients are nervous about what is going to happen and I like to reassure them, answer their questions and try to make the experience a little better for them. It can sometimes be challenging dealing with patients who are upset or angry, but it's rewarding to be able to help them.

When I finished Year 10, I applied directly to a hospital and trained as a ward assistant. Then I started training as a Division 2 Nurse, which I did for more than six years. After nursing I decided I'd like the challenge of being a ward clerk because of the variety in the work, which involves handling telephone enquiries, using computer records and dealing with patients.

A few words of advice:
You need to enjoy working with people to do this job.

ROBERT BAK
WARD CLERK

'You need to enjoy working with people'

RUNNING A HOSPITAL

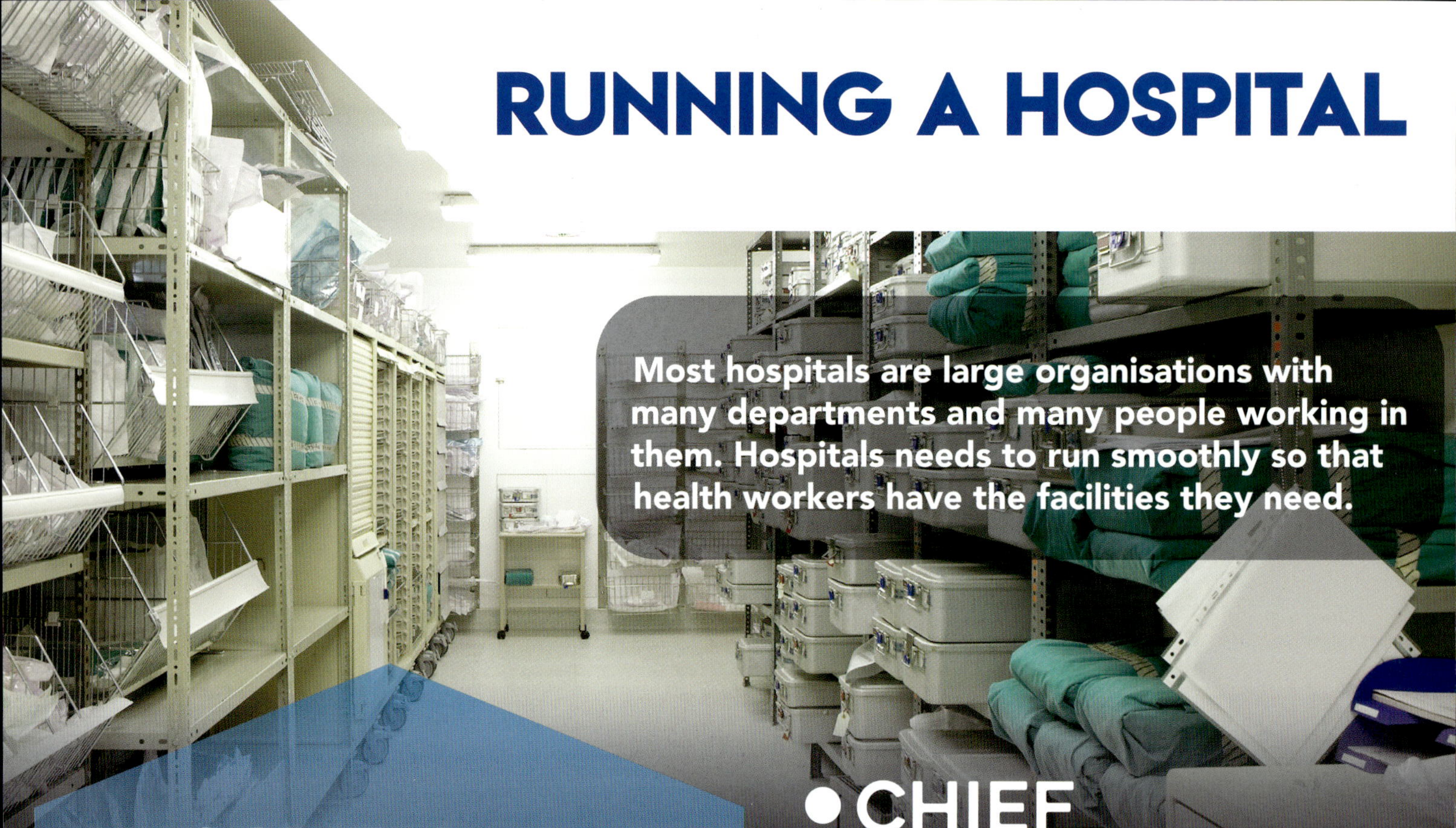

Most hospitals are large organisations with many departments and many people working in them. Hospitals needs to run smoothly so that health workers have the facilities they need.

HOSPITAL ADMINISTRATORS

JOB DESCRIPTION

Hospital administrators organise the running of a hospital. They enable the health professionals to provide the best care for their patients. These roles require different levels of qualifications and experience.

RANGE OF WORK:

- plan the distribution of staff in areas such as safety, maintenance, records and accounts
- liaise with medical and nursing staff to ensure the best and most appropriate services are provided

EDUCATION AND TRAINING

Hospital administrators work at many levels in all departments of a hospital. As a starting point, working in hospital administration has the same requirements as any business or office administration. As administrators take more responsibility, they usually need to have specific hospital experience or qualifications. There are certificate, diploma and degree courses at tertiary institutions that focus on the various areas and levels of hospital administration.

CHIEF FINANCIAL OFFICER

JOB DESCRIPTION

A large part of the financial administration of a hospital involves making sure there is enough money available. These funds come from government grants, doctor and patient fees and other sources, in order to pay for the costs associated with providing health services to patients.

RANGE OF WORK:

- develop budgets to meet the costs of purchasing and maintaining medical equipment, pharmaceuticals, cleaning, catering and staff
- arrange payments to contractors for building maintenance, new constructions
- arrange payment of utility bills such as telephone and Internet, electricity and water

EDUCATION AND TRAINING

TAFE certificate in accounting or office administration is a starting qualification, but a university degree in finance or commerce will be needed for senior positions.

MEDICAL RECORDS

JOB DESCRIPTION

The data from medical records provides information for allocating funds and developing budgets. This data gives medical and administrative staff information about patterns occurring in diseases, injuries and accidents. Public health authorities and medical researchers use this information for the health needs of the community.

EDUCATION AND TRAINING

Senior and management jobs in the medical records department will require tertiary education. Clerical jobs in medical records' departments don't require specific qualifications but general office training would be helpful.

CHIEF EXECUTIVE OFFICER

JOB DESCRIPTION

A hospital is usually managed by a Chief Executive Officer (CEO). The CEO works closely with a Board of Management made up of the heads of the various departments of the hospital, such as doctors, nurses, pharmacists, finance managers, caterers, record keepers and maintenance workers.

EDUCATION AND TRAINING

A CEO will usually have qualifications in hospital administration or business management as well as experience in hospital administration.

'I recommend this job for people who like to be organised'

MY STORY

After finishing Year 12, I decided to study health information management because I was interested in a job that involved being organised and structured, together with staff management. I did a three-year degree in Science (Health Information Management).

When I started my first job at St. Vincent's Hospital I was in charge of 15 staff. There was also opportunity for advancement as there were four grades of managers, the highest of which is my current job as Manager of Health Information Services. While working in this field for 12 years, I have completed a Graduate Diploma and am now studying for a Master's Degree in Health Administration. This extra study increases my understanding of other areas of hospital administration, as well as allowing me to make contacts with people from other hospitals.

A few words of advice:
I would highly recommend this job for people who like to be organised.

CAMERON BARNES
MANAGER, HEALTH INFORMATION SERVICES

DENTISTRY

There are many jobs that involve looking after people's teeth. Some dentists specialise in particular areas such as:

- paediatric dentistry – treat children
- orthodontics – straighten teeth
- periodontics – treat gums
- prosthodontics – artificially restore teeth and gums
- oral surgery – operate on the mouth and teeth

DENTIST

JOB DESCRIPTION

Dentists advise their patients on how to prevent tooth decay and gum disease by practising good oral hygiene and having a healthy diet. They check for any teeth and gum abnormalities, decay to teeth and any tooth cavities. They repair damaged teeth, fill any cavities and, if necessary, refer patients to dental specialists. Some dentists make dentures.

EDUCATION AND TRAINING

To become a dentist you must complete a degree course in dentistry at a university. Dentistry degrees can take up to five years and often involve clinical training in a dental hospital. To be accepted into the course you have to get very good marks at Year 12 level.

DENTAL TECHNICIAN

JOB DESCRIPTION

Dental technicians design and construct different kinds of artificial teeth such as dentures and crowns. Many dental technicians use Computer Aided Design in their work. Dental technicians work in dental hospitals or in laboratories. They work with dentists and dental specialists, and sometimes with patients as well.

EDUCATION AND TRAINING

Dental technicians usually undertake a TAFE course. Diplomas are also available and can often be completed at the same time as an apprenticeship.

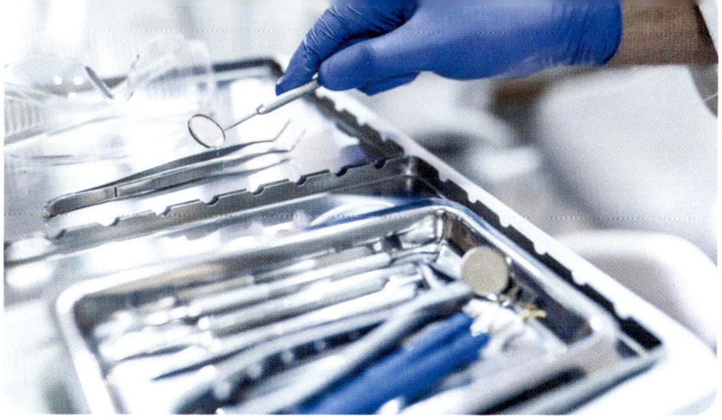

DENTAL HYGIENIST

JOB DESCRIPTION

Dental hygienists assist patients with their oral hygiene, explaining the best methods of brushing, flossing and plaque control. Hygienists apply various preventative treatments to teeth and gums. They also remove stains and polish teeth.

EDUCATION AND TRAINING

Dental therapists must complete a two-year diploma Dental therapists and hygienists need to study a relevant tertiary course in dentistry and must have completed year 12.

DENTAL ASSISTANT

JOB DESCRIPTION

Dental assistants help dentists to prepare and treat patients. Many dental assistants also act as receptionists.

RANGE OF WORK:

- clean, sterilise and prepare instruments for use by dentists
- record patient information
- help make patients comfortable
- send out bills and reminders
- make appointments
- greet patients on arrival

EDUCATION AND TRAINING

Most dental assistants have completed a certificate course at a TAFE institute.

MY STORY

I knew I wanted to become a children's dentist when I was five years old. My mother took me to several dentists for treatment, but we were turned away because I had serious dental problems. Finally my mother found a kind dentist who agreed to help us and he treated me for many years. When I was in Year 12, I was too shy to admit my plans to study dentistry to my dentist – it wasn't until I got into the dentistry course that my mother told my dentist that he had inspired me to be a dentist.

I did a dental degree at university, then a Master's Degree in paediatric dentistry while working at a children's hospital. I studied and taught in the United States for two years, before returning to Australia to work with another paediatric dentist. Now I have my own private practice.

One of the things I love about my work is seeing children happy to come to the dentist. I try to make it a positive experience.

A few words of advice:
If you want to be a children's dentist it's a good idea to get work experience working with children.

KAREN KAN
PAEDIATRIC DENTIST

'I try to make [visiting the dentist] a positive experience'

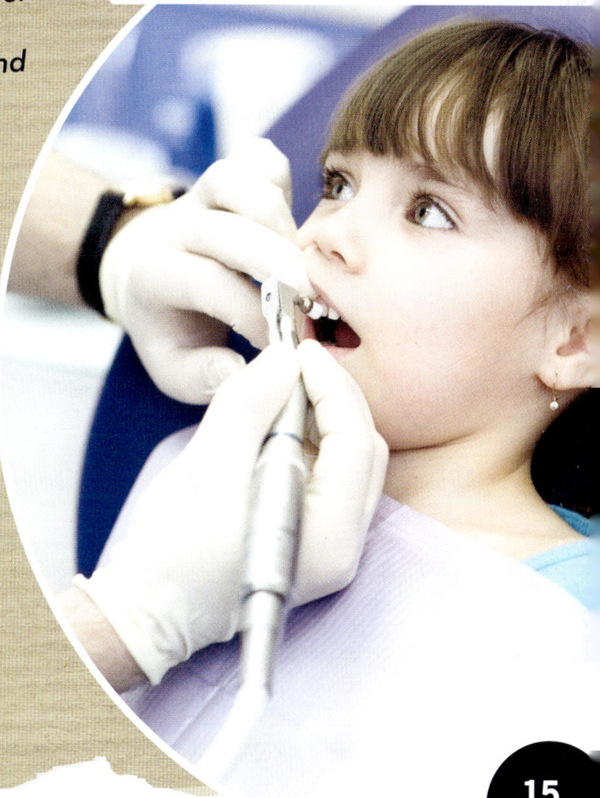

EYE CARE AND HEARING

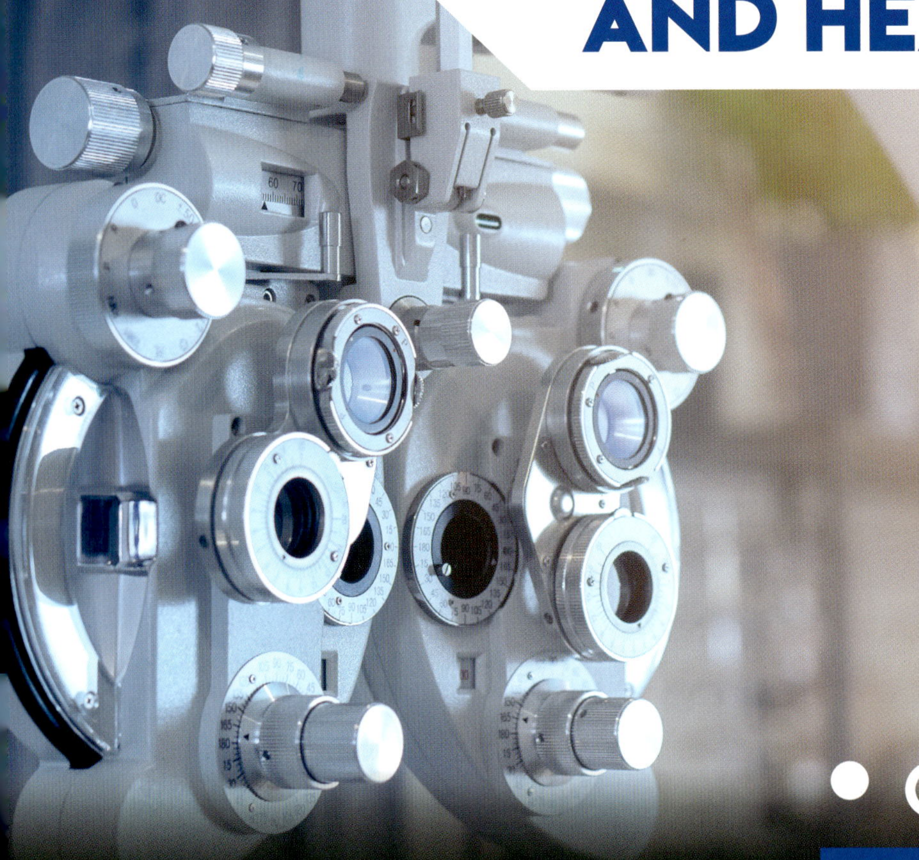

Our eyesight and hearing are very important. There are many occupations that involve looking after the health of people's eyes and ears, and treating a variety of sight and hearing problems.

OPTICIAN

JOB DESCRIPTION

Opticians are trained technicians who provide eyewear such as contact lenses and glasses. They use the instructions and information prescribed by optometrists and ophthalmologists. They help clients choose frames for glasses, fit lenses to the frames and assist with any required adjustments for client comfort. Opticians also advise their clients on the use of contact lenses.

EDUCATION AND TRAINING

Opticians must complete a relevant course of study at a TAFE college.

OPTOMETRIST

JOB DESCRIPTION

Optometrists examine eyes to diagnose and treat eye or vision problems. They check for the presence of eye diseases, and they prescribe and dispense glasses and contact lenses for their patients.
Optometrists also provide rehabilitation for visually impaired people, helping them to make the best use of the vision they have.
Optometrists may perform simple procedures and may prescribe medication for some eye diseases.
Major eye surgery and serious eye diseases are only treated by qualified ophthalmologists, who have studied this speciality further.

EDUCATION AND TRAINING

Optometrists must complete a degree course at university, which can take up to five years. Most optometry courses have a clinical component, where students examine and treat patients while being supervised by a qualified optometrist.

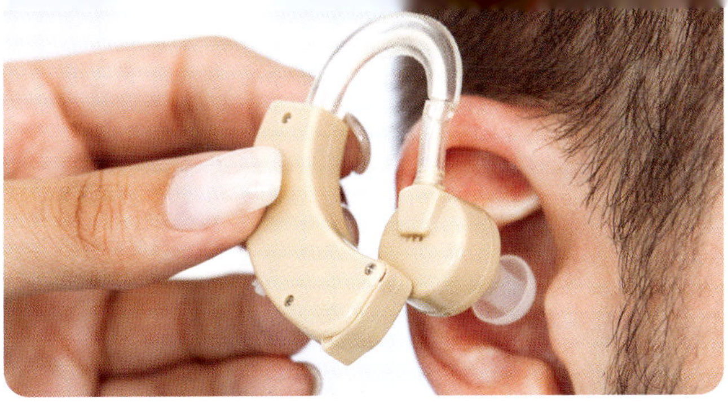

AUDIOLOGIST

JOB DESCRIPTION

Audiologists assess and manage hearing difficulties in adults and children. Where required, they prescribe and fit hearing aids and assist patients and their families with their use. Audiologists may advise industry about safe noise levels and steps for the prevention of hearing loss. They often work closely with audiometrists, teachers, social workers, speech pathologists, psychologists, doctors and ear specialists.

EDUCATION AND TRAINING

Audiologists need to have completed the relevant university degree, as well as practical training.

AUDIOMETRIST

JOB DESCRIPTION

Audiometrists perform hearing tests for audiologists and are involved with fitting hearing aids and giving advice on their use. They can also work in industry advising on appropriate hearing protection devices and measuring noise levels to assess potential hazards for employees.

EDUCATION AND TRAINING

Audiometrists need to have completed tertiary studies which include a health sciences degree. Often, post-graduate study is also required.

MY STORY

'our work is always varied and interesting'

I can remember finishing high school and not having a clear idea of what I wanted to do. I did work experience with my local optometrist and decided that optometry was something I would enjoy.

I didn't get in to an optometry course after school so I started a science degree. I did the same subjects as optometry students and at the end of the year I transferred into the course. My first job was in a rural area, where I got to treat a wide variety of eye diseases and visual problems. There is always a demand for health workers in rural areas and the experience is really valuable.

For the last four years I have worked in a practice in the city. We have the very latest technology and our work is always varied and interesting.

CLAIRE JACKSON
OPTOMETRIST

A few words of advice:
Spend at least a year working in rural Australia. It's both for you and the community.

MOVING SMOOTHLY

Physiotherapists, podiatrists and occupational therapists all provide treatment that focuses on the body's ability to move around. Their work involves treatment that helps people to rehabilitate after injury or to strengthen the body to prevent injury.

• PHYSIOTHERAPIST

JOB DESCRIPTION

Physiotherapists help people who are having difficulty with movement because of injury or disease. Physiotherapists work in hospitals, rehabilitation centres, disability care, aged care, sports clinics, fitness centres and private clinics. They may also specialise in the care of specific patients such as the aged, young children, expectant and new mothers, or sportspeople.

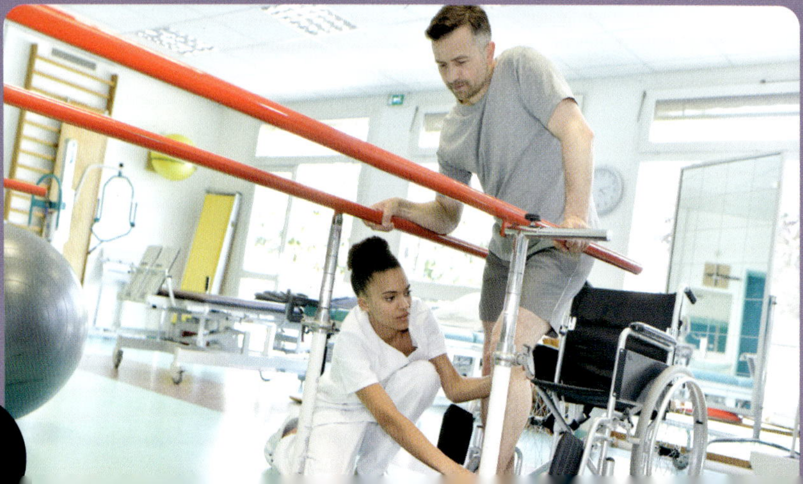

RANGE OF WORK:

- treat patients with heat and ice packs, massage, ultrasound and electrotherapy, exercise and hydrotherapy
- help patients with rehabilitation programs
- give advice on ways to prevent injury through strengthening exercises and the correct use of various parts of the body

EDUCATION AND TRAINING

Physiotherapists must complete a university degree such as a Bachelor of Physiotherapy. Candidates must be interested in science and the human body as they will need to study the functions of all the muscles, joints and bones. Physiotherapists must also be physically fit enough to lift and manipulate heavy body parts.

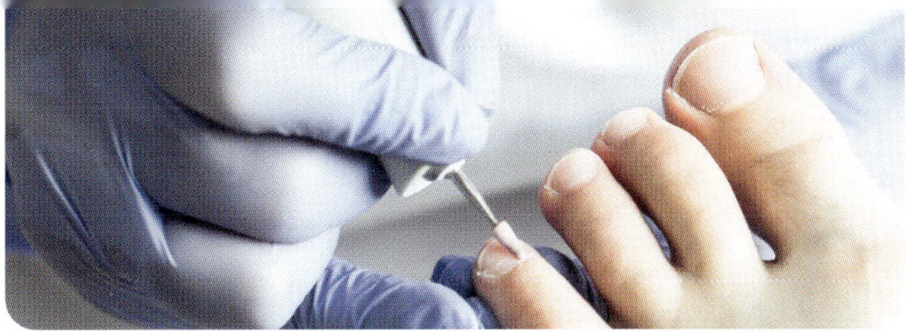

PODIATRIST

JOB DESCRIPTION

Podiatrists deal with the prevention, diagnosis and treatment of foot problems, as well as the rehabilitation of the feet after injury. They treat conditions that may be caused by bone and joint disorders, or are the result of neurological or circulatory diseases. Podiatrists also manage skin and nail disorders, foot injuries and infections. They may act as consultants to industry or footwear manufacturers.

RANGE OF WORK:

- advise patients on preventative health, such as appropriate footwear for work that involves standing for long periods of time
- treat injured feet and pre-existing foot problems

EDUCATION AND TRAINING

Podiatrists must complete a four-year university degree course, such as a Bachelor of Podiatry.

OCCUPATIONAL THERAPIST

JOB DESCRIPTION

Occupational therapists (OTs) help people who have disabilities. People who were born with a disability or who became disabled following illness, injury or accident can be treated by an occupational therapist to achieve as much independence and mobility as possible. OTs assess patients' capabilities, and help them to gain the skills necessary for day-to-day living.

RANGE OF WORK:

- work in hospitals, rehabilitation centres, aged or disability care centres, prisons and private clinics
- assess patients' injuries and capabilities
- work with assessment teams to assess people's abilities to live independently

EDUCATION AND TRAINING

To become an occupational therapist you need to complete a university degree in a relevant field of health science.

MY STORY

I decided to be a physiotherapist when I was a teenager. I was a tennis player representing Victoria and I watched the tennis squad's physiotherapists working. Being interested in science and people, I thought it was the perfect combination for me. I still have an association with tennis, and I work every year at the Australian Tennis Open, treating injuries and supervising training. I'm a consultant to Tennis Australia, assessing young players in order to design training programs that increase strength and help prevent injuries.

I work with my business partner in a private physiotherapy practice. We treat a variety of patients, including sportspeople, people who've been involved in accidents at work or on the road, and residents of local nursing homes. I enjoy my work because I love helping people to recover.

A few words of advice:
You need to be fit and active to be a physiotherapist because the job is very physically demanding.

JOANNA MEAGHER
PHYSIOTHERAPIST

'You need to be fit and active'

SPEECH, FOOD AND EMOTIONAL HEALTH

A person's health can be greatly influenced by everyday habits. Many medical conditions can be avoided or controlled by eating an appropriate diet, the way we think and feel can have a huge impact on our physical health, and the way we speak can affect our success in many areas of life.

• PSYCHOLOGIST

JOB DESCRIPTION

Because of the great variety of jobs within the profession of psychology, many psychologists choose to specialise in one area. Psychologists use many techniques, including counselling and psychotherapy, to treat a wide range of mental and emotional health issues.

RANGE OF WORK:

- provide counselling to people who are experiencing emotional difficulties
- provide assessment and advice in legal cases involving criminal behaviour
- provide advice on learning and developmental problems in educational settings
- diagnose, assess and treat mental illness and psychological problems

EDUCATION AND TRAINING

Psychologists need to have completed a university degree course approved by the Australian Psychological Society. Most psychologists also undertake postgraduate study in a specialised area.

• DIETITIAN

JOB DESCRIPTION

Dietitians use their expertise in nutrition to advise on the importance and effects of the foods that people eat.

RANGE OF WORK:

- give advice to people with specific dietary needs such as sportspeople, people with allergies and diabetics
- write articles on food for magazines
- work as consultants to food manufacturers, catering departments, schools and hospitals

EDUCATION AND TRAINING

Dieticians must complete a university degree course in a relevant area of applied science or nutrition and dietetics.

SPEECH PATHOLOGIST

JOB DESCRIPTION

Speech pathologists help patients who have difficulties with oral communication. These difficulties may be the result of accident or illness, some hearing loss, or problems with childhood language development.

RANGE OF WORK:

- work in a variety of places including kindergartens, schools and universities, nursing homes, hospitals, rehabilitation and community health centres, or in private practice
- work with a team of professionals such as teachers, nurses, doctors, social workers, occupational therapists and physiotherapists

EDUCATION AND TRAINING

To become a speech pathologist you need to complete a university degree related to speech pathology and undertake practical training.

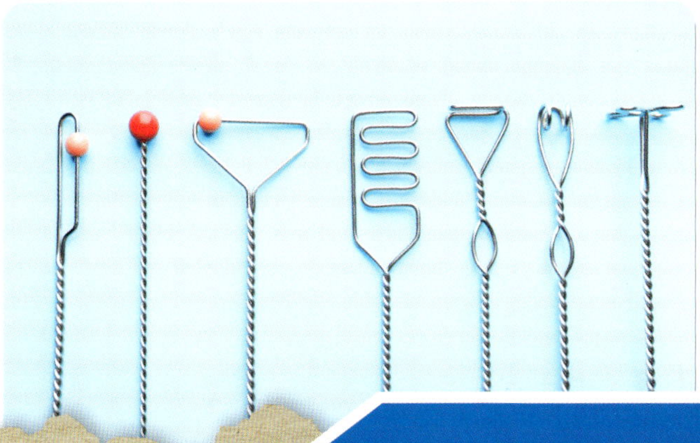

MY STORY

When I was about 20 years old and studying science at university, I discovered that I wanted to be a dietitian. I liked finding out how and why things worked, such as the human body. I had a passion for nutrition and dietetics. I loved finding out little things like: bread crusts don't really make your hair curly but carrots actually can help you to see better.

I work as a dietitian in a hospital where I provided special diets for patients. By giving different foods, I can help people's wounds heal, or help people with food allergies. I also teach people about the sorts of foods they should eat if they have a condition such as diabetes. Working with doctors, nurses and other staff also makes this job very interesting.

One of the best things about being a dietitian is that you can work in range of environments - in a hospital, for a food company, in a laboratory producing foods, or be involved in getting health messages out to the public.

A few words of advice:
Work experience is one of the best ways to see if you would like this career. Contact some dietitians and find out what your local options are.

ERICA CLIFFORD
DIETITIAN

'find out what your local options are.'

PHARMACISTS

A pharmacist's job is to supply, dispense and manufacture medicines. Pharmacists can work in a variety of places, such as pharmacies in shopping centres, in hospital pharmacy departments, for pharmaceutical manufacturers, or for the Government, advising on which medicines can be used in Australia.

COMMUNITY PHARMACIST

JOB DESCRIPTION

In community pharmacies, pharmacists dispense medicines with the appropriate directions for their use. They give advice to both patients and doctors on the best way to take the medicines and on any side-effects. Pharmacists also provide information about health promotion and the prevention of diseases. A community pharmacist may also sell a lot of products and provide services that are not health related. Some pharmacies sell toys, clothing, cosmetics and even lottery tickets. A lot of a pharmacist's time can be taken up with providing free advice, so the sale of additional products and services can help to keep the business financially stable.

HOSPITAL PHARMACIST

JOB DESCRIPTION

The role of a hospital pharmacist is to provide medicines for patients in the hospital, and to monitor their usage. They give advice to patients and health professionals regarding the medications they dispense. They may also be involved in trialling medicines and preparing them for patients to use.

PHARMACEUTICAL COMPANY PHARMACIST

JOB DESCRIPTION

A pharmacist working in a pharmaceutical company does not have much contact with patients, but works like a scientist doing research to develop new or improved medications. They may also work in the marketing of the company's products to medical professionals and community pharmacists.

EDUCATION AND TRAINING

Pharmacists must complete a pharmacy degree at university, then work under supervision as a pharmacist for one year.

HEALTH PROMOTION

Health promotion involves finding ways to make people think differently about the ways that they can keep themselves and others healthy. This can mean finding new ways to expose common health problems, and helping people to find solutions that work for their individual situations.

• HEALTH PROMOTION OFFICER

JOB DESCRIPTION

Health promotion officers work for private and Government organisations to educate and encourage people to lead healthy lifestyles and prevent disease. Examples of such organisations are QUIT, the Cancer Council and the National Heart Foundation.

RANGE OF WORK:

- plan and conduct public awareness and education campaigns through the media
- design and distribute material for the public and for use in schools
- carrying out research
- release research findings related to health and disease prevention

EDUCATION AND TRAINING

Health promotion officers come from a range of backgrounds. Some have specific health promotion training, but many have worked as nurses, health educators or teachers.

PE TEACHER

JOB DESCRIPTION

Most Australian high schools and many primary schools employ trained physical education (PE) teachers to instruct students in sports, recreational activities and personal health and safety.

RANGE OF WORK:

- plan and prepare a yearly teaching program
- teach the basic techniques of a range of individual and team sports
- teach students about personal and community health
- teach students about personal development
- teach students a range of safety practices

EDUCATION AND TRAINING

PE teachers need to have completed a teaching degree and to have studied PE.

'really believe in your goals'

MY STORY

I worked as a student welfare officer and as a health teacher before joining QUIT – the organisation that aims to reduce smoking levels in the community. My job involves designing activities to reduce smoking amongst young people. Together with others at QUIT, I develop activities and materials to carry the anti-smoking message. I work with schools, local councils and community health centres and have also advised researchers and overseas government health departments in India, Japan, Britain and Canada.

The variety of people I meet in my work is one of the things I love about this job. I really feel like I am doing something worthwhile. The results of my work in preventing smoking may not be seen for decades, but I know it will save people's lives.

A few words of advice:
You don't see the people you are helping face to face, so you have to really believe in your goals and believe they will be achieved in the future.

IAN FERRETTER
HEALTH PROMOTION OFFICER

EMERGENCY RESPONSE WORKERS

Responding to emergency calls and treating injured or critically ill people is a very demanding job. There are teams of people with different roles who work together to provide emergency health services to the community. Ambulance officers, paramedics and communications officers work with other emergency service workers such as firefighters, police and search and rescue teams.

• PARAMEDICS

JOB DESCRIPTION

Paramedics help people in emergencies by treating them before and during transport to hospital for further treatment. Paramedics also attend big public events so they are readily available in case of accidents. In emergency situations, paramedics usually work in a team of two, so one member can drive while the other treats the patient. The job is often traumatic and the personal support that team members give each other is very important.

EDUCATION AND TRAINING

There are various courses at tertiary level that provide entry to paramedic work.

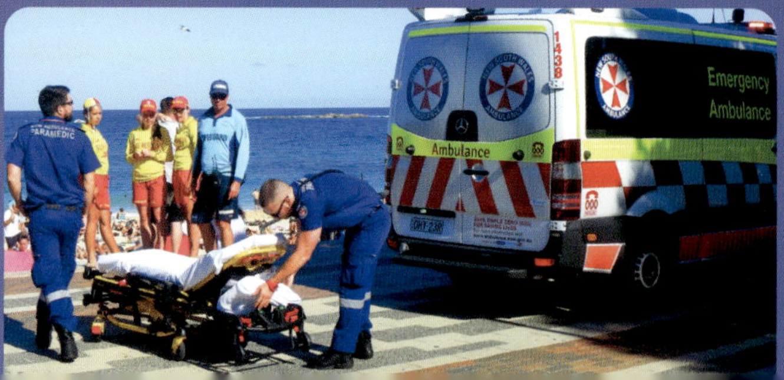

COMMUNICATIONS OFFICERS

JOB DESCRIPTION

Ambulance officers can also work as communications officers. They work in the control centre that sends out ambulances in response to emergency calls. Their emergency training is very useful to be able to understand and appropriately respond to the emergency needs of patients.

SEARCH AND RESCUE

JOB DESCRIPTION

Paramedics and ambulance officers may also work as a part of search and rescue teams in remote areas. Such work requires special training in rescue techniques, as well as emergency care skills.

MY STORY

After I completed my university degree in biochemistry, I wasn't sure what I wanted to do. I wanted work that was exciting, involved problem-solving and the outdoors. I took some time off from studying and went for a skiing holiday in Canada. There, I saw the ski patrols who attend injured skiers. That's when I decided I wanted to work as an ambulance officer. When I came back to Australia I applied to the ambulance service. I was immediately accepted and received on-the-job training while I completed a diploma in Health Science.

As a paramedic I attend accidents and answer emergency calls from patients needing hospital treatment. I work day and night shifts. One of the great things about my work is that I see it all – from delivering babies to helping someone who is dying. My work makes me feel I am doing something that makes a real difference to people's lives. Helping people is extremely satisfying – this is absolutely the best job in the world.

A few words of advice:
You need to be adaptable to work in emergency situations, and be able to think quickly and calmly.

KATE CANTWELL
AMBULANCE PARAMEDIC

'be able to think quickly and calmly'

MEDICAL TECHNOLOGISTS

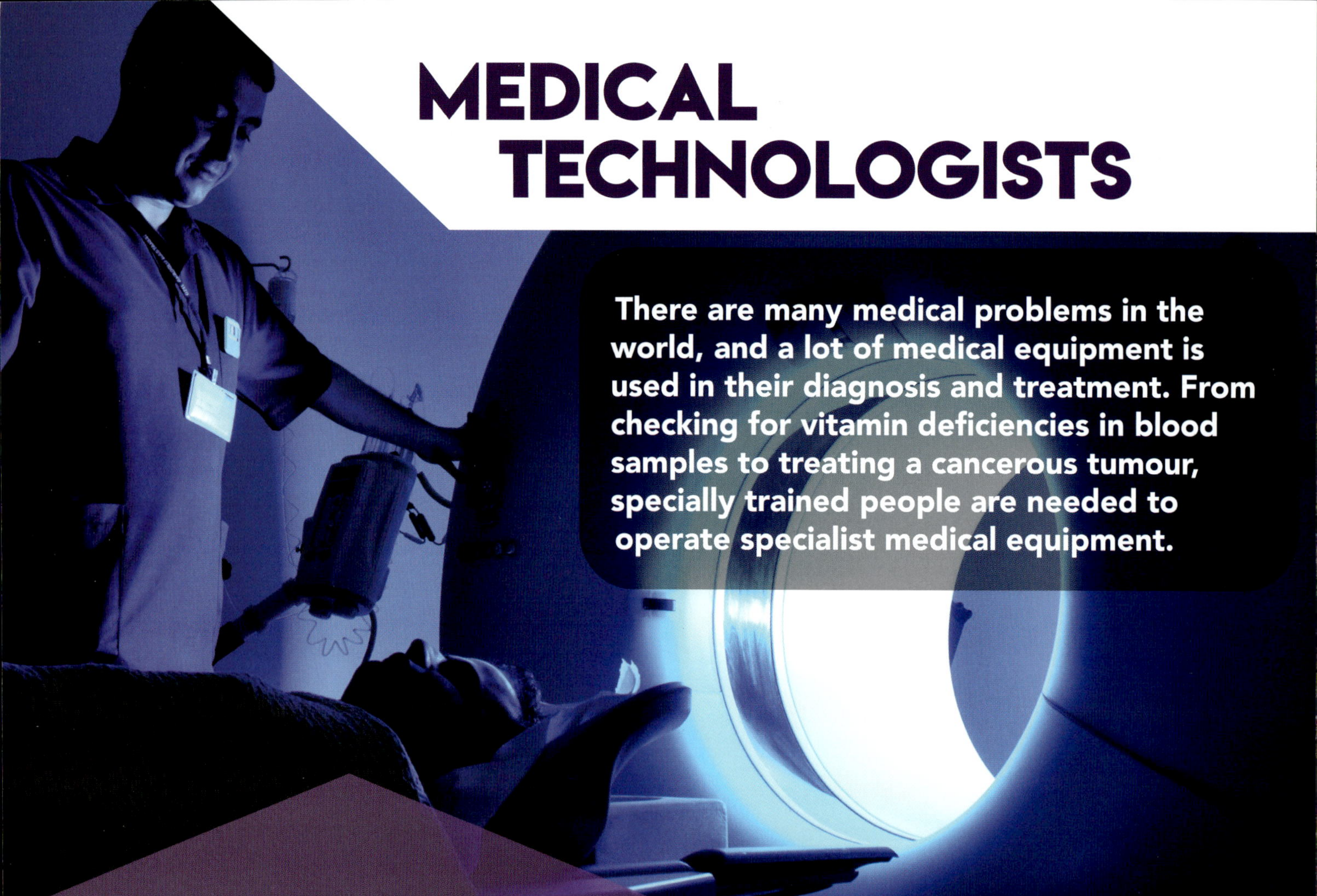

There are many medical problems in the world, and a lot of medical equipment is used in their diagnosis and treatment. From checking for vitamin deficiencies in blood samples to treating a cancerous tumour, specially trained people are needed to operate specialist medical equipment.

RADIATION THERAPIST

JOB DESCRIPTION

Radiation therapists operate the machines that are used to apply radiation to treat some forms of cancer. They work with oncologists (specialists in cancer treatment) and radiologists (specialists in radiation therapy) to determine the strength and type of beam to be used, depending on the size and location of the tumour. They have a lot of contact with patients and guide them through treatment at what is usually a very stressful time.

EDUCATION AND TRAINING

To become a radiation therapist you need to complete a relevant university degree and gain practical experience.

MEDICAL IMAGING TECHNOLOGISTS

JOB DESCRIPTION

Medical imaging technologists (also called diagnostic radiographers) use hi-tech machines and techniques including radiography, x-ray and ultrasound to provide diagnostic images of the internal parts of the body. Medical imaging technologists work with doctors, specialists and nursing staff in hospitals and clinics.

EDUCATION AND TRAINING

To become a medical imaging technologist you need to complete a relevant university degree and gain practical experience.

MEDICAL LABORATORY TECHNICIAN

JOB DESCRIPTION

Medical laboratory technicians conduct tests and other procedures to assist in the diagnosis and treatment of illnesses or abnormalities. They test human samples including tissue, blood and body fluids in order to detect the presence of infections, diseases or disorders. The test results are interpreted by a pathologist (a medical doctor who has specialised in diseases) and are reported to the health professionals who requested the tests. Medical laboratory technicians usually work in hospital pathology departments or in private pathology practices. They may also work in medical research centres and universities.

EDUCATION AND TRAINING

To become a medical laboratory technician, you need to complete a TAFE course or have a similar qualification.

MEDICAL SCIENTIST

JOB DESCRIPTION

Medical scientists conduct and analyse laboratory tests and samples from humans in order to diagnose, treat and prevent disease. They may prepare samples for different kinds of testing and carry out research in order to find out more about the nature of certain diseases and find improvements for treatment.

They work in hospitals, medical research centres, universities, pharmaceutical companies and Government health departments. Working in medical science involves lots of research and laboratory work.

EDUCATION AND TRAINING

To become a medical scientist you need to complete a university degree as a minimum qualification.

'tests you are doing could save someone's life'

MY STORY

I always liked biology and chemistry at school, and looking at things through a microscope. While I am interested in diseases and the human body, I've never liked the thought of actually working directly with patients. I finished Year 12 and did a two-year diploma in laboratory technology (pathology) at TAFE, then I got a job in a hospital. Some people think it's unpleasant working with some of the materials I look at, but I think it's fantastic that you can find out so much information about someone's health by examining their blood or whatever. It's a bit like a detective looking for clues to solve a mystery.

I prefer working in a hospital because you are directly helping patients being treated in the hospital. Lab technicians can also work in universities doing research, but I like knowing that what I do could be helping someone immediately.

A few words of advice:
As a lab technician you are often working on your own. You need to be able to be accurate, even under pressure, because the tests you are doing could save someone's life.

STEPHEN RINALDI
MEDICAL LABORATORY TECHNICIAN

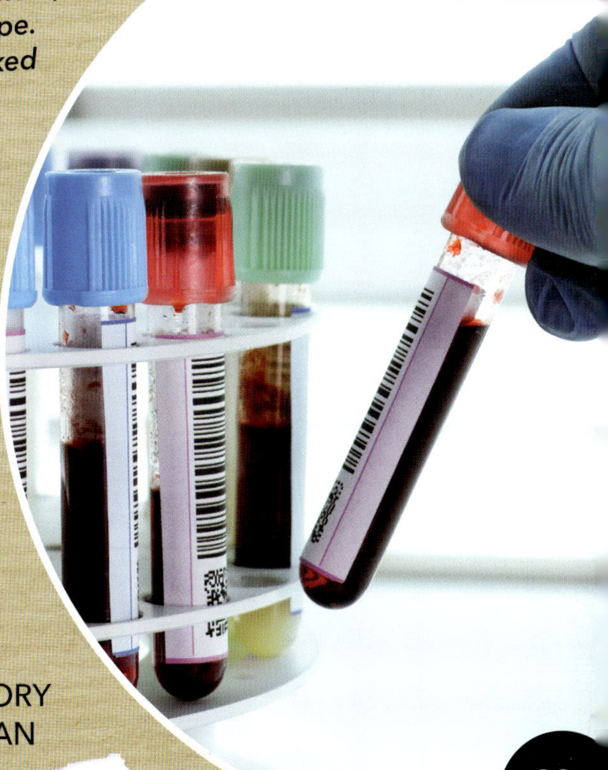

GET FUTURE READY

If you think you might be interested in a career in health, there are a few things that you can do right now that might be useful later. Why not research your education pathways to see what options are available to you. Maybe you could plan the qualification route that you might like to follow, or investigate the practical steps you could take to gain experience in the types of work that interest you.

THE FUTURE

PRACTICAL EXPERIENCE

- join a volunteer community service group such as Surf Life Saving Australia or the Rural Fire Service
- take a first aid course and volunteer as a first aid provider at school or at your workplace
- volunteer at your local aged care facility
- get work experience in a local health care setting

DO YOU NEED QUALIFICATIONS?

Skilled health care workers are becoming increasingly valued in the wake of a global pandemic. If you are interested in working in patient care, it's important to start developing a good bedside manner. It can even be worthwhile learning a different language (or two) to be able to care for patients who may not speak English.

There are courses at universities and TAFE colleges that specialise in the large range of health care jobs available today and into the future. The health care industry is growing rapidly and is attracting large numbers of applicants. Anything you can do to make yourself stand out from the crowd will not only help you, but could make the world of difference to your patients one day.

GLOSSARY

administration day-to-day processes involved with running a business or office

cavities hole in a tooth, caused by decay or acid erosion from food

crown cap over a tooth, or an artificial single tooth

degree three to four-year course of study through a university

dentures plate with one or more false teeth

diagnose use knowledge to understand and communicate what is wrong with a person

diploma one to two year course of study through TAFE or university

electrotherapy electrical currents that stimulate muscles and tissue to heal

hydrotherapy exercise in water

impaired weakened or damaged in some way

pharmaceuticals medicines and substances used to diagnose and treat illness and medical conditions

plaque sticky build-up on teeth where bacteria can multiply

prescribe use medical knowledge to give authority to purchase regulated medications

preventative used to stop injury from happening or illness developing

rehabilitation process of restoring the body to its pre-illness or pre-injured state

suturing sewing skin or other body parts back together after it has been cut or torn

TAFE Technical and Further Education

INDEX

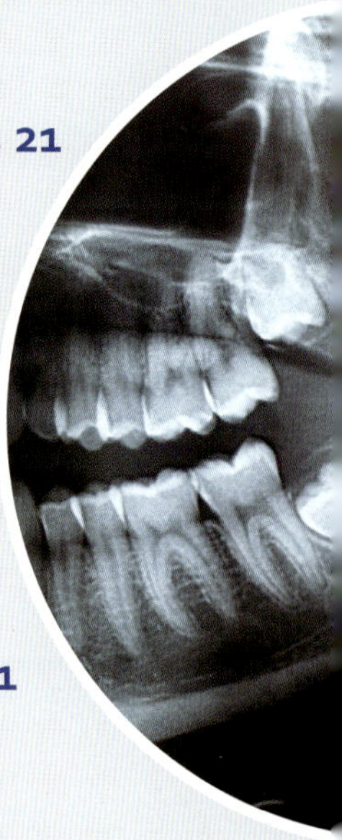